IN THE ZONE

LACROSSE

DON WELLS

MEDIA ENHANCED BOOKS

AV2 BY WEIGL

ADDED VALUE · AUDIO VISUAL

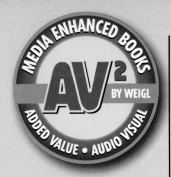

MEDIA ENHANCED BOOKS
AV² BY WEIGL
ADDED VALUE • AUDIO VISUAL

BOOK CODE

G 8 3 0 4 7 6

AV² by Weigl brings you media enhanced books that support active learning.

AV² provides enriched content that supplements and complements this book. Weigl's AV² books strive to create inspired learning and engage young minds for a total learning experience.

Go to **www.av2books.com**, and enter this book's unique code. You will have access to video, audio, web links, quizzes, a slide show, and activities.

Audio
Listen to sections of the book read aloud.

Video
Watch informative video clips.

Web Link
Find research sites and play interactive games.

Try This!
Complete activities and hands-on experiments.

Due to the dynamic nature of the Internet, some of the URLs and activities provided as part of AV² by Weigl may have changed or ceased to exist. AV² by Weigl accepts no responsibility for any such changes. All media enhanced books are regularly monitored to update addresses and sites in a timely manner. Contact AV² by Weigl at 1-866-649-3445 or av2books@weigl.com with any questions, comments, or feedback.

Published by AV² by Weigl
350 5th Avenue, 59th Floor
New York, NY 10118
Website: www.av2books.com   www.weigl.com

Library of Congress Cataloging-in-Publication Data available upon request.
Fax 1-866-44-WEIGL for the attention of the Publishing Records department.

ISBN 978-1-61690-018-2 (hard cover)
ISBN 978-1-61690-019-9 (soft cover)

Printed in the United States of America in North Mankato, Minnesota
1 2 3 4 5 6 7 8 9 14 13 12 11 10

052010
WEP264000

PROJECT COORDINATOR Heather C. Hudak   DESIGN Terry Paulhus

IN THE ZONE

CONTENTS

■ Lacrosse is a game of speed, skill, and physical strength.

Lacrosse is North America's oldest team sport. During the 1600s, French **missionaries** in what is now Canada watched American Indians play a game called baggataway. Baggataway was played to train warriors, settle disputes between tribes, and during ceremonies. The missionaries called the game "la crosse" because the head of the stick players used resembled the cross **bishops** carried.

Baggataway teams often had between 100 and 1,000 players. A large rock or tree was used as the goal. The two team's goals were usually 500 yards

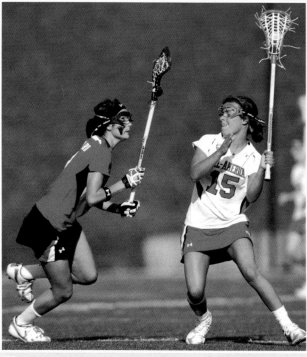

More than 5,500 women play lacrosse at 240 U.S. colleges and universities.

(457 meters) apart. Sometimes, they were several miles apart. Players scored by hitting the goal with a ball or by hitting the ball between goalposts. American Indian lacrosse games could last two or three days.

A Canadian dentist named W. George Beers introduced the first modern set of lacrosse rules. He determined the size of the playing field, the number of players on each team, and other basic rules.

Lacrosse has been played in the United States since the 1880s. At that time, lacrosse was played mostly at colleges along the east coast of the United States. It has slowly grown in popularity across the country. Today, people in more than 20 countries play lacrosse.

Lacrosse can be a rough game. Players need special equipment to prevent injuries while playing lacrosse.

Men wear helmets with face guards. The helmet and face guard protect players from face and head injuries.

Lacrosse players wear mouth guards to protect their teeth.

Players wear jerseys in their team colors. Jerseys are loose to allow players to easily twist their bodies and swing their arms.

Players wear gloves to protect their hands.

Male players wear shorts. Female players often wear skirts.

Lacrosse players wear shoes called **cleats**. The shoes help players grip the ground and prevent slipping. When playing indoors on concrete, players wear sneakers.

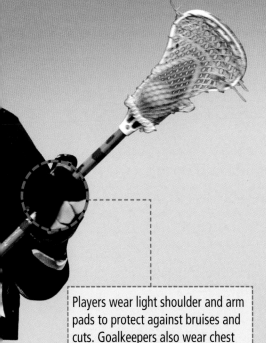

The lacrosse ball is hard rubber. It measures about 2 inches (6 centimeters) across and weighs about 5 ounces (142 grams).

■ Lacrosse balls are made of hard rubber and are often white or orange.

Players wear light shoulder and arm pads to protect against bruises and cuts. Goalkeepers also wear chest protectors and pads that cover their groin, shins, thighs, and elbows.

Each player uses a stick, or crosse, with a hook at the end. The hook is crossed with cord to form a small net, or pocket. Players use the stick to catch, carry, and throw the ball. Only the goalkeeper can touch the ball with his or her hands.

■ The goalkeeper's lacrosse stick has a larger head and pocket than the sticks used by other players.

■ Lacrosse sticks can be made of wood, aluminum, or titanium.

Outdoor lacrosse is called field lacrosse. It is played on a rectangular grass field. Women usually play on a larger field than men. There is also an indoor version of lacrosse called box lacrosse. Some indoor leagues play on **turf**. Others play on concrete.

Goals are set up at each end of the field. A crease is marked on the field around each goal. Only the goalkeeper is allowed in the goal crease. The offensive and defensive zones are large boxes around the crease.

A centerline divides the field in half. Each end is marked with a centerline flag. The center of the field is marked with an "X." Flags also mark each corner of the playing field. They help players easily see the field's boundaries. The boundaries are called sidelines and end lines.

■ The lacrosse goal has two 6-foot (1.8-m) poles attached at the top by a 6-foot (1.8-m) crossbar.

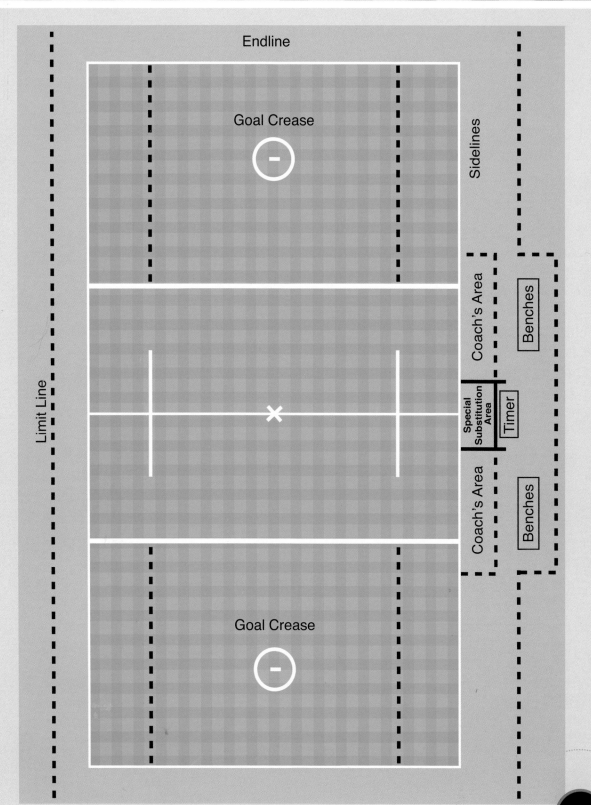

College lacrosse games are 60 minutes long. High school games last 48 minutes. Games are divided into four quarters, with a 10-minute rest period between halves. At the end of the game, the team with the most goals wins the game. If the score is tied at the end of the game, men's teams play four-minute overtime periods to break the tie. The first team to score in an overtime period wins.

Women's teams play two three-minute overtime periods. The team that scores the most goals in overtime wins. If the game remains tied, they play until one team scores.

Players use lacrosse sticks to carry and pass the ball. The stick has a hook at the end that is strung with rawhide, **gut**, **nylon**, or linen cord to form a pocket that can hold the ball.

■ The referees use their hands to direct the lacrosse game.

All players can run with the ball. A player controls the ball by cradling it in the stick's head. Players pass the ball by flicking the stick forward. Players can pass the ball in any direction.

Players rarely attempt long passes because long passes often go out of bounds or are picked up by opponents. Usually, players run as far as they can before passing the ball to a teammate. Players make short, quick passes around the goal. They hope to move the defenders out of position and create gaps in front of the goal.

■ Coaches help players understand the game and play their best. They also carry out a game plan.

Physical contact is only allowed in men's lacrosse. Players use contact to stop their opponents and force them away from the goal. Players use their sticks to check, or hit, the ballcarrier's stick to knock the ball from the pocket.

Play stops if the ball goes out of bounds or a **penalty** is called. When a player scores a goal, play also stops. Play does not stop if the ball hits the ground.

■ Men's lacrosse can be a very rough game. This is why players wear protective padding, a mouth guard, and a helmet.

Box lacrosse teams have one goalkeeper and five runners. All runners play **offense** and **defense**. In women's lacrosse, each team has a goalkeeper, three offensive players, five midfielders, and three defensive players. Each men's field lacrosse team has a goalkeeper, three defensemen, three midfielders, and three attackers.

One of the midfielders is called the center. The center takes the face-offs that begin each period. The center and midfielders play offense and defense. They bring the ball forward to the attackers or help the defensemen guard the goal.

Attackers usually have the best stick-handling skills. Midfielders are usually the fastest players on the team. Defenders are usually quick, strong players.

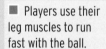

■ Players use their leg muscles to run fast with the ball.

■ When the ball is close to the goal, players rush to help their goalkeeper.

Play begins with a face-off at the center of the field. The official blows a whistle, and each center tries to gain control of the ball.

Each team must always have at least four players on the defensive side of the field and three on the offensive side. If a defensive player carries the ball over the centerline, another player must step back to the defensive side of the field. A team that has more than three players on the offensive side of the centerline is called offside by the referee.

■ The goalkeeper is the last line of defense when a player from the opposing team is trying to score a goal.

In a men's lacrosse game, players can check with their bodies or sticks. Women are only allowed to hit the stick of a player carrying the ball.

Male players can use their body to hit an opposing player carrying the ball or any opponent within 15 feet (5 m) of the ball. This is called a body check. Body checks must be made above the waist and from the front or side, never from behind. This rule reduces the chance of serious injury.

Players can use several methods to knock the ball from the pocket of the opponent's stick. They can hit their stick against their opponent's stick. They can poke their stick at a ballcarrier's hands. They can also slap the ballcarrier's hands.

In women's lacrosse, a check happens when a player uses her stick to hit an opposing player's stick.

A penalty is called when a player commits the following fouls. The referee calls a personal foul when a player trips another player, makes an aggressive check, or makes an illegal body or stick check. A technical foul is called when a player pushes or holds an opponent, touches the ball with his or her hands, or goes offside. An expulsion foul is called if a player is too aggressive when hitting an opponent or uses abusive language with an official. A player who commits an expulsion foul is removed from the game.

■ In men's lacrosse, tackling opponents is common.

Players who break the rules must serve a penalty for a certain amount of time. The player who received the penalty must leave the field. The team must play with one less player until the penalty is over or a goal is scored. The length of time that a player sits out varies according to the type of foul called.

■ When certain fouls are committed, a penalty flag is thrown.

Lacrosse has some well-known legends. They entertained fans and broke records.

Jim Brown

BIRTH DATE: February 17, 1936
POSITION: Midfield
CAREER FACTS:

- Brown is considered one of the greatest players in college lacrosse history. He is also known as a great football running back.
- In high school, Brown won three all-star honors for playing midfield.
- Syracuse University recruited Brown to play lacrosse.
- Brown was an **All-American** in 1956 and 1957.
- Brown was elected to the Lacrosse Hall of Fame in 1983.
- Brown is currently an advisor to the Cleveland Browns.
- Brown also runs a program called Amer-I-can, which helps kids in inner cities stay out of gangs.

Paul Gait

BIRTH DATE: April 5, 1967
POSITION: Midfield
CAREER FACTS:

- With his brother, Gary, Paul Gait helped lead Syracuse University to three straight National Collegiate Athletic Association (NCAA) lacrosse championships from 1988 to 1990.
- Gait won the National Lacrosse League's (NLL) Most Valuable Player award in 2002.
- Following a serious foot injury, Gait retired when the 2002 season ended. He returned to play National League Lacrosse in 2005. He played four games with the Colorado Mammoth.
- In 2005, Gait and his brother were inducted into the United States Lacrosse National Hall of Fame.
- In 2006, Gait became head coach of the Rochester Knighthawks, a team in the National Lacrosse League.

Casey Powell

BIRTH DATE: February 18, 1976
POSITION: Attack

CAREER FACTS:

- Powell was a four-time All-American at Syracuse University.
- In 1995, with Powell's help, Syracuse won the 1995 NCAA National Championship.
- In 2005, Powell was named Major League Lacrosse (MLL) Offensive Player of the Year.
- Powell is ranked second in all-time assists in Major League Lacrosse.
- The record for the most all-time points in Major League Lacrosse is held by Powell.

Kelly Amonte Hiller

BIRTH DATE: December 31, 1973
POSITION: Center

CAREER FACTS:

- Hiller was a four-time All-American in lacrosse at the University of Maryland.
- In 1995 and 1996, Hiller was named NCAA Division I Lacrosse Player of the Year.
- Hiller helped the University of Maryland Terrapins win the 1995 and 1996 NCAA Division I Lacrosse National Championships.
- Hiller was a member of the 1997 and 2001 World Championship Women's Lacrosse Team.
- In 2002, Hiller became head coach of women's lacrosse for the Northwestern University Wildcats.
- Under Hiller, the Wildcats have enjoyed a 0.822 winning percentage, five NCAA national championships, and five NCAA conference titles.

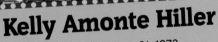

The stars of today are thrilling fans and drawing more people to lacrosse.

Ryan Powell

BIRTH DATE: February 23, 1978
POSITION: Attack

CAREER FACTS:
- Powell was a four-time All-American at Syracuse University.
- Powell began playing Major League Lacrosse in 2001.
- In 2001 and 2006, he was voted Most Valuable Player.
- In 2006, Powell won the Offensive Player of the Year Award.
- Powell's brothers, Casey and Mike, are also lacrosse superstars.
- Since 2001, Powell has played in the National Lacrosse League.

Kristen Kjellman

BIRTH DATE: November 18, 1984
POSITION: Midfielder

CAREER FACTS:
- Kjellman began playing for the Northwestern University Wildcats in 2004.
- She is the only Northwestern student to score 50 or more goals per season for four straight years.
- The Wildcats won three national NCAA titles in a row during Kjellman's time on the team.
- Kjellman won the 2006 and 2007 Tewaaraton Trophy. The trophy is presented to the top varsity collegiate players in the United States.
- She won the Honda Sports Award for Lacrosse in 2005, 2006, and 2007.
- Kjellman is a three-time American Lacrosse Conference Player of the Year.

Mark Millon

BIRTH DATE: May 17, 1971
POSITION: Attack

CAREER FACTS:

- Millon was a three-time All-American at the University of Massachusetts.
- In 2001, Millon was named Major League Lacrosse All-Star Game Most Valuable Player.
- Millon was named Major League Lacrosse Offensive Player of the Year in 2002 and 2003.
- In 2005, Millon was named Major League Lacrosse Most Valuable Player.
- Millon tied with Casey Powell for most single-season points in 2007, scoring 305 points.
- Millon formerly played nine seasons for various teams in the indoor National Lacrosse League.
- In 2007, Millon became a player for the Long Island Lizards in Major League Lacrosse.

Gary Gait

BIRTH DATE: April 5, 1967
POSITION: Midfielder

CAREER FACTS:

- Gary Gait was a four-time All-American at Syracuse University.
- In 1988 and 1990, Gait was named NCAA National Player of the Year.
- Gait achieved the third most career goals and the second most goals in a single season at Syracuse University.
- He set the NCAA lacrosse tournament record for most goals, with 50 goals in 11 games.
- In 1991, Gait joined the National Lacrosse League. He won the league's Most Valuable Player award six times.
- Gait scored 61 goals in the 2002-2003 season, breaking his own record of 57 goals, set in 1988.
- Gait is in both the United States Lacrosse National Hall of Fame and the National Lacrosse League Hall of Fame.
- In 2007, Gait returned to Syracuse University to become head coach of the women's lacrosse team.
- Gait re-entered Major League Lacrosse, signing on as an attack with the Toronto Nationals for their first season in 2009.

Lacrosse is a physically demanding sport. Eating a healthy diet and practicing other types of exercise will help athletes enjoy lacrosse.

A healthy diet helps keep athletes strong. Eating foods from all of the food groups every day will keep a player's body in top condition. Grain products, fruits, and vegetables provide necessary vitamins, minerals, and fiber. Calcium keeps bones strong. Dairy products provide calcium. Meat provides protein to build muscles.

■ Almonds are an excellent source of protein.

■ Vegetables provide nutrients the body needs to keep healthy and active.

Drinking plenty of water before, during, and after lacrosse is important. Water keeps people's bodies cool. When lacrosse players sweat, they lose water. Drinking water replaces what is lost through sweat during a game.

Strong, flexible muscles are important for lacrosse players. Stretching keeps muscles flexible and prevents injuries. It is best to stretch during and after a **warmup**. Running in place for a few minutes or running a few laps warms and loosens the body's muscles.

■ Playing lacrosse uses many muscles. A player must stretch his or her entire body to prevent injuries.

Lacrosse Brain Teasers

Test your knowledge of this fast-paced sport by trying to answer these lacrosse brain teasers!

1 Who invented the game of lacrosse?

2 Where did the name for lacrosse come from?

3 What is the main difference between a goalkeeper's stick and a player's stick?

4 What special kind of shoes do lacrosse players wear to help them grip the ground and prevent slipping?

5 What happens if the ball hits the ground?

6 How long is the rest period between halves in a lacrosse game?

ANSWERS: 1. American Indians invented the game of lacrosse. 2. The name of the game came from the shape of the lacrosse stick, which resembled the cross (la crosse) that bishops carried. 3. The main difference is the size of the stick. The goalkeeper's stick has a larger head and pocket. 4. The special shoes worn by lacrosse players are called cleats. 5. If the ball hits the ground, play continues as normal. 6. The rest period between halves is 10 minutes.

Glossary

All-American: selected and honored as a sport's best amateur player or athlete in the United States

bishops: people who oversee many churches

cleats: special athletic shoes with small spikes on the bottom; this may also refer to the spikes themselves

defense: the players trying to prevent the other team in a game from scoring

gut: a strong cord made from the intestines of sheep

missionaries: people sent by religious groups to spread their religion in another country

nylon: a human-made fabric

offense: the players trying to score in a game

penalty: punishment for breaking the rules

turf: artificial grass or field made of human-made material

warmup: gentle exercise to get a person's body ready for stretching and game play

Index

Log on to www.av2books.com

AV[2] by Weigl brings you media enhanced books that support active learning. Go to **www.av2books.com**, and enter the special code inside the front cover of this book. You will gain access to enriched and enhanced content that supplements and complements this book. Content includes video, audio, web links, quizzes, a slide show, and activities.

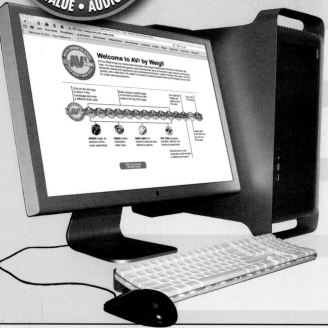

Audio
Listen to sections of the book read aloud.

Video
Watch informative video clips.

Web Link
Find research sites and play interactive games.

Try This!
Complete activities and hands-on experiments.

WHAT'S ONLINE?

Try This! Complete activities and hands-on experiments.	**Web Link** Find research sites and play interactive games.	**Video** Watch informative video clips.	**EXTRA FEATURES**
Pages 6-7 Test your knowledge of lacrosse equipment.	**Pages 4-5** Find out more information about the history of lacrosse.	**Pages 4-5** Take a video tour through the history of modern lacrosse.	**Audio** Hear introductory audio at the top of every page.
Pages 8-9 See how well you know a lacrosse field.	**Pages 8-9** Learn more about the lacrosse field.	**Pages 18-19** View an interview with one of the world's top lacrosse players.	**Key Words** Study vocabulary, and play a matching word game.
Pages 12-13 Test your knowledge of lacrosse positions.	**Pages 10-11** Learn more about playing lacrosse.		**Slide Show** View images and captions, and try a writing activity.
Pages 16-17 Write a biography about one of the superstars of lacrosse.	**Pages 12-13** Read about lacrosse positions and players.		**AV[2] Quiz** Take this quiz to test your knowledge
Pages 20-21 Play an interactive game.	**Pages 14-15** Learn more about the rules of lacrosse.		
Page 22 Test your lacrosse knowledge.	**Pages 20-21** Find out more about eating well.		